I Do, I Will, I Shouldn't Have

Single, dating, married, and then divorced

You tried it the world's way and your way, but what about God's way?

Copyright Instructions

I Do, I Will, I Shouldn't Have

Unless a person is explicitly identified by name, the statements that are used should not be directly attributed to any specific person.

Unless otherwise marked, all scripture quotations are referenced from the New King James Version of the Bible.

ISBN-10: 0989087832
ISBN-13: 978-0-9890878-3-4

Printed in the United States of America.

Published by Kingdom Journey Press
A Division of Kingdom Journey Enterprises, Woodbridge, VA
www.kjpressinc.com

Cover Design by Brand U Inc.
www.branduinc.com

Dedication

This book is dedicated in loving memory of my cousin Tobi, who passed away on December 24, 2011 from pancreatic cancer. She was a single parent of two children, but never married. Both of our mothers experienced divorce before we were teenagers. I used to ask myself if our mothers had married men who came from the Lord. I am not sure they did, but I believe that had their husbands come from God, perhaps they would not have gotten divorced, because divorce does not come from God!

I also dedicate this book to everyone who has a desire not to repeat past mistakes.

This book is also dedicated to those who are looking for love in all the wrong places. Whoever said experience is the best teacher lied! Experience is not always the best teacher and can kill you! Know that you can learn from someone else's mistakes.

Last, but not least, I dedicate this book to my ex-husband, Christopher Edward Suydan, for all the lessons I learned from him.

The steps of a good man are ordered by the Lord;
and he delighteth in his way.
Psalm 37:23

Table of Contents

Introduction

I Do, I Will, I Shouldn't Have is an inspirational relationship guide for single Christian women who desire to be married, as well as those who are divorced because they married someone who was not the person that God intended for them. These guidelines will serve as teaching tools and will encourage the reader to follow God's plan for their life through His Word.

This book is a testimony of how God kept my mind through my own self-inflicted storms. It is a guide which is designed to encourage, empower and inspire you, the reader, to allow God to lead you in every decision on every level and area of your life. ***I Do, I Will, I Shouldn't Have*** describes my regret for bad choices and mistakes I made as a single Christian woman. Perhaps it will also aid you to look back over past relationships, choices, decisions, and habits and consider what you could have done differently.

Prayer will get you through your journey of trials and mistakes and help you to understand that you are still valuable to God! Know with assurance that Jesus has your back and He will carry, guide, and keep you if you will only seek, trust, and obey Him when making major life decisions.

Everything we go through matters to God. He loves us and only wants the best for us! Jesus has a purpose for each of us and we are gifted to do His will. We do not have to threaten our relationship with Jesus for one-night stands with people who are not good for us. It is not worth our souls to abort our purpose in Christ just to please the flesh, but even if we do fall, we do not have to give up because we have messed up. God has made a way for us to repent. Rise and perform the will of the Lord for your life!

Reader Discretion is Advised!

Chapter 1 – How We Met

Joined together February 23, 1995

I Do, I Will, I Shouldn't Have!

Marriage is a beautiful union, but we can marry the wrong person, and our lives can be turned upside down!

Mirror, mirror on the wall, being married to the wrong person can cause us to fall!

Fall where?

Being married to the wrong person can cause us to fall into depression, sadness, and even into a vengeful state of mind. It can cause us to fall far away from God. It may even cause us to fall into someone else's arms while still married. This is not the plan God has for us.

My husband and I dated for nine months before getting married. I learned this was too short a time to commit to someone you barely know. Unless, of course, God has spoken directly to you and said this person is to be your husband or wife, do not allow yourself to go there.

We met during our Army Reserve weekend rifle range training.

I should have been aware of Chris when we met and he was sitting there in his Army uniform, looking innocent. The weekend of our reserve training was very dreary, cold, and rainy. I remember riding on the back of a military truck with my friend Judy. All of a sudden, I heard someone using a lot of profanity. It was Chris, cursing up a storm.

I blurted out, "Boy, you need Jesus!"

Everyone on the truck got very quiet for a second until Judy said, "Girl, stop telling everybody they need Jesus!"

I looked up at Chris, wondering if he was going to give me a piece of his mind. He said, "You are right, I do need Jesus."

Judy and I looked at each other with a sigh of relief and just laughed.

While Chris and I were talking, we discovered we had a few things in common. We had both been on active duty for seven years in the U.S. Army and were now serving four years in the U.S. Army Reserve. We both were Dallas Cowboy fans, we loved to eat, and we enjoyed comedy. This was all we had in common.

Chris was a class clown, too. He was always cracking jokes, and he enjoyed making everyone laugh.

As we stood in the cold rain, he and I continued our conversation as the "food truck" came driving by with hot drinks and hot food. Chris excused himself from our conversation and walked over to the food truck. He walked back over to Judy and me, giving us cups of hot chocolate so we could warm up a little—our Army ponchos were not preventing us from getting wet from the cold rain as they were designed to. Anyway, Judy and I thought that was very generous of him. After we thanked him, I thought to myself "Now that is a true gentleman." Little did I know that was the beginning of my journey through the tests of time!

~The Difference in How We Were Reared~ Our Childhood Background

It is very important to know how your potential mate was raised.

Chris and I were reared very differently. He was born and reared in Washington, D.C. but acted as if he had been raised in the Deep South. He was very country in style. He was the youngest of four children. He began telling me a little about school and why he decided to join the U.S. Army to become a Communication Cable Operator.

Chris shared with me how he began doing chores at a very young age. By the age of nine, he was preparing his own food because his mom worked the night shift at the County Hospital. He told me he got whippings for being a bad child! I do not believe children are bad, but just a little curious. Chris was not allowed to participate in any sports or activities that may have caused him to get physically hurt. He also was not reared in a church; having a spiritual foundation is very important and can make all the difference.

I was a city gal, born and reared in North Philadelphia. After graduating from Kensington High School, I enlisted in the U.S. Army to become a Telecommunication Operator and to get away from the city life for a while. I was not ready to attend college, so I thought the Armed Forces was the next best thing. I am the only daughter of four children. I never dated until after I moved away from home.

My mom is the second of eleven children, and she was very hard on my brothers and me. She seemed to be harder on me because I was the only girl. Because she reared us in church, it felt as though we lived there. Church was our life; there was church and more church. We had services on Sunday for the entire day, from Sunday school at 10 AM, regular Sunday service at 11 AM, and either a 4 or 7 PM service. We went back on Tuesday for prayer and Bible study. We had service and midnight prayer on Friday. There was a big difference in what I was exposed to versus what Chris was exposed to, and what a difference it made in our marriage.

For some reason, I had more chores to do than my brothers, and I never understood why. I felt like boys needed to know how to clean and cook, too! I never understood why my mom would tell one of my brothers to mop the floor or wash the dishes, and when they did not do what she asked, she would call out my entire name and say, "Towhanna Arlette Boston, wash the dishes and mop the kitchen floor."

I would say, "I thought you told John to wash the dishes and mop the floor."

She would say "I did, but now I am telling you to do it."

I thought to myself, "This is so not fair!"

Mom was convinced that I went into the military to get away from home, but I was just ready to venture out on my own. Although mom was extremely strict, I appreciate my upbringing and having a mom who cared. There were many things I did not understand then, such as chores, manners, and curfew. I do understand now and found myself instilling some of those same values into my children.

CB

Chapter 2 – Dating

Prior to leaving our weekend reserve training at Fort Meade, Chris and I exchanged telephone numbers. This was my first mistake. As a Christian woman, I should not have given Chris my telephone number, let alone gone on a date with him. Why? Because he was not ***saved,*** and what communion hath light with darkness?

II Corinthians 6:14 — *"Be ye not unequally yoked together with unbelievers: for what fellowship hath righteousness with unrighteousness?"*

The second mistake was not praying and asking God to save him and whether he was the man for me. Oh, how I found out the hard way that Chris was clearly not the man God had chosen for me. Do not get me wrong, I believe God can bring a person off the streets, clean them up by saving them, and prepare them just for you, but Chris and I were traveling down two completely separate paths.

I remember growing up listening to my mom say, "You made that bed for yourself. Now lie in it." In other words, you brought that situation upon yourself, and now you have to deal with it. Obedience is much better than sacrifice, and because I stepped out of God's will for my life, there was a very heavy price to pay.

The following week, our first date was going to church. Somebody say, "It was a set up!" Afterwards, Chris and I also began going out to eat, attending a few comedy shows, and occasionally going to the movies. Did I know to do better? Of course, but my biological clock was ticking fast and all I could think about was becoming somebody's wife. I was 34 years of age and a single parent with two daughters. Becoming someone's wife would have given me that complete family that I longed for. Also, it would have ended my inconsistency in maintaining my celibacy off and on. I would do good maintaining for six months, or sometimes longer, and then begin dating again, but before I knew it, I was back to square one. I continued struggling with fornication because I continued setting myself up for failure by dating unsaved men. I fell short one too many times and needed complete deliverance from this weakness.

My daughters were six years apart by two different men and were born during my seven years of serving on active military duty. Neither of my daughters' fathers was active in their lives when I began dating Chris. By then, my older daughter was a teenager attending middle school.

After the first five months of dating, my girls and I went to visit my mom for Christmas in Philadelphia, and I asked Chris to pick us up. When my mom met Chris, she said "Girl, you better not marry him! Leave that one alone, because something is just not right with him!"

Parents can see directly through their children's relationships and have the wisdom we need, and most of the time they are right about what they perceive to be bad for us, but there are times when they are wrong. The price for our disobedience can be so damaging that we may never recover.

I remember when my cousin Tangy had dated a young guy, and when her mother met the young man, she could instantly sense trouble. She was not wrong about him. She told Tangy not to date him because something was just not right. Well, as adults, we just do not want our parents telling us what to do, even if they are right. Tangy did not listen, and after dating this young man for a little over a year, she began to see exactly why her mother pleaded for her not to date him. Tangy tried to break off the relationship. Instead of letting her go, he had the mentality that "if I cannot have you, then nobody will." He became very angry and ended up killing Tangy. What a heavy price to pay for disobedience.

If you find yourself dating or interested in someone, pray first. Make your request known unto God. The reason it is suggested that you pray first is because although God has given us free will, just as He has given you the choice to become born again by accepting Jesus Christ as your Savior, He is also giving us the opportunity to allow Him to order our steps when selecting our mate or making life-changing decisions. **Psalms 37: 4–5**: *Delight thyself also in the Lord; and he shall give you the desires of thine heart. Commit thy way unto the Lord; trust also in him; and he shall bring it to pass.* So as we seek God for our mate and anything else in life, it has to first start with delighting ourselves in the Lord! There is a very clear way to discern whether this is the person for you. One who has accepted Christ as their Lord and Savior can distinguish the voice of God versus their own voice, and that is through daily communication with Him. The closer you get to the Lord through the meditation of His Word, the clearer His voice will become. But while waiting, here are some steps that may help in knowing the voice of God versus your own heart's desire, whether you are a babe in Christ or a seasoned saint:

- Awareness – be aware of your prayer life and hiding the Word in your heart to ensure spiritual growth is evident while monitoring the advice of others.
- Alertness – pay close attention to your surroundings and the company of others who may not have your best interests at heart, which can become a distraction.
- Availability – Being available to receive from the Lord all He has promised to you.
- Remain focused on ministry, and if you are already dating, take time to really get to know his or her family, friends, and neighbors to observe their view of this person. Also, when dating someone, as you take time getting to know them, learn how they were reared. Can they cook and clean? How does this person handle money? Most importantly, ask yourself, "Is this the man or woman God intends for me to marry?"
- Be honest and true to yourself.
- Remain very clear and consistent in your communication, meaning: Do not say one thing with your mouth and demonstrate something totally opposite with your actions, confusing the relationship.

Also, part of the responsibility of a child of God in being able to distinguish God's voice is understanding their pastor, teacher, minister, or leader of their place of worship and what is being taught. Stop for a moment and ask yourself "what am I being taught?" A woman should be taught to hide herself (commit her ways, trust in Jesus), and the man should be taught to seek the Lord with all he has. Now, if this man or woman is not saved, run!

These are very important values when you are considering spending the rest of your life with someone, until death do you part! Keep in mind that a person's environment and how they are reared have a lot to do with how and why they make decisions.

When dating, we may see several red flags, but we often ignore them because of wanting to see the good in the person. Even if the man or woman is saved, it is very important for the relationship to be ordained by God, because people sometimes play a lot of mind games, even within the church. People are going to be people, and we all make mistakes, but why must men and women play these silly emotional games within the church? For example, a man shows interest in you and would like to take you out to dinner, while at the same time you overhear him asking another woman out who also attends your church. You bring it to his attention, and he acts as if he does not know what you are talking about. Another example is when a man within your church has your number and email and acts as if he really likes you, but does not want anyone in church to know he is interested. He only wants to deal with you behind closed doors. What is that about? You really do want who God has for you!

If you are already married, prayer is a powerful tool for keeping your marriage. Prayer will help you push forward, keeping God first and at the center of attention in your life, as well as in the center of your marriage.

Chapter 3 – Hidden Agendas

If you are a woman and share your number with a person that you have decided to date without first seeking the approval of the Lord, you must be aware that there may be some hidden agendas. Now if this person is in fact from God, you should not have to be concerned with any hidden agendas. I do not believe God will set us up with somebody who is jacked up from the floor up.

Perhaps you are a single woman with children, and the man you decide to date has a hidden agenda to get close to one of your children instead of getting close to you! We are responsible for protecting our children, and the person may not really want us, but may really be after our sons or daughters.

How often is it that we hear on the news about a child being molested by a woman's boyfriend or friend? God will not give us someone to date and marry who would harm us or our children. We do not serve a God who will set us up to be harmed. We must know that God will not set us up with a person who will bring destruction to our lives, but picking someone on our own could very well put us in great danger. God always has our best interests in mind.

We should not just pursue a man because he is cute, handsome, fine, or can sing. He may stand in front of the mirror longer than you do! It is not just about looks, and this handsome man may be in love with himself and not really in love with you. Pray and share with the Lord the qualities you would like in a man, and make sure he has a job!

II Thessalonians 3:10 — *"If any would not work, neither should he eat."*

A dear friend of mine who was a single parent of two children became very involved in the choir and attended weekly Bible study. She began dating a very handsome, young man who was not saved. Once they began dating, I started noticing that she was not coming out to Bible study as much anymore, and she began missing choir rehearsals. She stopped singing and stopped attending Bible study to pursue this fine looking man. I asked her if everything was alright. She told me about the gentleman and how well he treated her. I shared my story of being married to Chris and explained to her that she could be headed down a bad path. About six months later, she and this man married. After they were married, she returned to church with her husband. Perhaps she thought she could change him and get him to give his life to Christ.

We often make the mistake of thinking we can change a man. Most of the time they end up pulling us away from the Lord simply because the relationship was not from God. Needless to say, her new husband did not become saved, and things did not happen as she had planned. She realized she had made a huge mistake. He began cheating on her, and she became very overwhelmed with the marriage. I have not spoken to her in quite some time, and I am unsure how the marriage is going now, or even if they are still married.

It is so important for us to follow the Word of God and believe what it says. How can two walk together except that they agree, and what fellowship does light have with darkness? We must believe that God knows who and what is best for us!

Now, Christian brothers, if you are a single dad and find yourselves dating women who God did not put you in a relationship with—someone who does not have children or does not want any—please be watchful. She very well may not like your child. Perhaps her plans may be to ship your kid off to boarding school the first chance she gets, just so she can have you all to herself or worse. Keep in mind that a woman's coke-bottle shape can be temporary; the body often changes after a couple of children and stress. Women beware, because perhaps that good-looking man is looking for a trophy wife. He may want to marry your body, but not the whole you. ***Pray, pray, pray!***

I Thessalonians 5:17 tells us to "pray without ceasing," meaning this should be the constant attitude of every Christian who is seeking directions, guidance, and communion with God.

There are a lot of marriages within the church that were established by individuals themselves and not by God! If a marriage is not established by God, it may or may not survive the storms of life that will come to shake the very foundation of the love you have for each other. God knows who and what is best for each of us! I believe we can specifically know whether our mate came from the Lord if He speaks to our hearts and shows us the individual.

Example: one of our Sunday school teachers shared how she and her husband met. They became really good friends, and that is all there was between the two. One day, he told her that God had shared with him that she would become his wife. She laughed and said, "I do not think so." After some time went by, she was praying, and God spoke to her heart to let her know that this man was to be her husband. After hearing this testimony, I became more convinced that God will show us who to marry.

Christian dating or courting should not be like the world dating system, with folks changing from one person to another. The Word of God lets us know that we are in the world but not of this world. God's way is not for us to date a person and break up six months later, only to start dating a different person. It is not His will for us to hop from person to person! When we are emotionally hurting due to breakups, it is very difficult for us to focus on the ministry God is calling us to serve. Bouncing around from Christian sisters to Christian sisters or Christian brothers to Christian brothers is not how God wants his saints to behave. One reason is because after accepting the Lord as our Savior, we are to begin practicing celibacy until marriage. The second reason is we should not continue practicing sin by fornicating.

Also, the brothers in the church should not be players juggling two or three women at a time. Do not be shocked and surprised, because it does happen right in the church. ***There will be absolutely no players, gigolos, or pimps in Heaven***!

I believe it can be a blessing having someone who shares your values, but more importantly, someone who shares your faith!

All disobedience is sin! If you are saved and living for the Lord, please know that whatever your struggles are, God is able to deliver and will set you free from every obstacle in your life. I am a person who enjoyed having sex. Once I became saved, that was a stumbling block in my life. The devil could not tempt me with cigarettes, beer, or even clubs, but a tall, handsome, well dressed, good smelling man was my weakness. I had to pray for the Lord to help me, because this type of man would have me melting like hot cheese on a grilled sandwich. Now I am giving God all the glory, because Jesus showed me He is a keeper and will keep anyone from sin through the Word if we allow Him to. We should not allow ourselves to be set up for failure. I would like for us to be encouraged as we do exactly as the Word of God instructs us to do. I believe that it may not be such a bad idea if we are dating a saved man or woman to go out in groups and not alone. This will help prevent us from being set up to fall into sin.

We often sit back and judge our Christian brothers or Christian sisters who have fallen into sin. Instead, we should be praying for their deliverance. Often saints will gossip and treat people very unkindly because of their lapses. Let us be encouraged to be very careful how we handle the faults of others when they fall, especially when they come to us for help.

The church is a hospital for the sick. We all have something that is not Christ like that we struggle with, such as lying, backbiting, overeating, or coveting. There is no big sin or little sin, because all *sin* is *sin.*

I am reminded of the scripture of **St. Matthew 7:3: "Why beholdest thou the mote that is in thy brother's eye, but considerest not the beam that is in thine own eye?"** Think about this question just for a minute. In other words, sweep around your own front door before you try to sweep around someone else's.

To that woman out there who was never married but has a baby out of wedlock, you have nothing to be ashamed of, because we all have sinned and fallen short of the glory of God. Jesus did not bring you this far to leave you where you are. There will be many mixed views and opinions from family, friends, and strangers regarding your situation. The key is to ask God to forgive you and ask Him for wisdom, guidance, and strength to bounce back.

When it comes to dating, you have your child to think about. The well-being and happiness of your child comes first, and though it can become hard taking care of your child as a single parent, you are equipped to survive. Do not be afraid to ignore those close to you who refuse to support, pray, and encourage you. If the absent parent does not want to have anything to do with you or the child, do not be afraid to apply for child support, because children cannot live off air. This journey of caring for this little person will not be easy, and the child needs you to focus on their needs. There will be times when you are feeling alone, but reach out to people within your support system. If they have abandoned you, then you have no choice but to pray your way through, asking God for help. You can still obtain your dreams and God's will for your life while caring for your child. Take one day at a time. After getting through that day, prepare yourself for the next day. There will be times within those days you may have to take one hour at a time, but you can and will make it. Don't give up.

There was a young sister in Christ who had been gifted with a beautiful voice. The Lord allowed her to minister to so many in songs. She was already a single parent, and after traveling from church to church performing in concerts, she became pregnant again and had a baby out of wedlock. This happens so often with too many sisters in the church. Now, some saints will support and pray with a sister that this happens to, and some saints won't. Some sisters continue ministering, and some don't. Whoever is the spiritual guide or advisor may encourage sisters to continue moving forward and not to give up ministering, but I want to pose a few questions regarding this matter: Should the pastor sit the sisters down? If so, what good would that do by sitting her down from ministry? Without justifying the sin when someone falls, it is important to show a lot of love.

I am remembering when I was a member of Church of Deliverance COGIC in Germany; I told the pastor that I was expecting, and he knew I was not married. He and his wife prayed with me. They did not have to sit me down from the choir and usher board, because I sat myself down. You might ask yourself why I sat myself down. Well, we had a few older teenagers; you might think kids are not watching, but they are. I did not want them to think it was okay to sin and still function in ministry as if nothing has happened. We must sincerely repent and ask God to help us to forgive ourselves.

The most important key is to develop a strong desire to please Christ by praying every day and studying the word of God. Be encouraged to walk in obedience. Perhaps you have had a setback because of sin. If you fall, get back up and try again. I do not believe in practicing sin, but I have learned over the years that it takes a strong determination to press past those things that are tempting and displeasing to God! The scripture says in **Romans 3:23 that "all have sinned, and come short of the glory of God."** The Lord knows that we are not perfect, but Jesus has given us every tool we need to live free from sin. Remember, there is never an excuse for practicing sin!

CB

Chapter 4 – Dating Websites and Matchmaking Games

Should Christians participate in dating games, such as speed dating?

First, what is speed dating? Speed dating is a formalized matchmaking process or dating system whose purpose is to encourage people to meet a large number of new people in the hopes of finding the right man or woman. What happened to praying and believing that God has a man or woman for us?

I do not believe that speed dating was created for the church and the saints of God, because I believe we are to pray for our mates to come from the Lord!

Philippians 4:6 — *Be careful for nothing; but in everything by prayer and supplication with thanksgiving let your requests be made known unto God.*

If we are seeking God and all of His righteousness, why would we need to find our mates on a dating website or playing a dating game? What in the world is happening to the church?

II Timothy 3:4 —*for men shall be lovers of pleasures more than lovers of God.*

My Christian brothers and my Christian sisters, allow the Lord to match make you!

St. Matthew 6:33 — *But seek ye first the kingdom of God, and his righteousness; and all these things shall be added unto you.*

If we are seeking God and all of his righteousness, that man or woman will be added unto us. We cannot go wrong following and standing on the promises of God!

Nowhere in this verse does it say to seek a mate by interviewing this man or woman to see if this is the person for us. The man or woman you are interviewing could be crazy as all outdoors. Lights are on in this person's mind, but no one is home. The person may be totally out of their God-given mind and completely unstable, but you have no way of knowing that for sure. I believe this is how the unsaved meet and date, and we have brought this way of dating into the church. Dating websites such as www.christianmingle.com and www.faithmate.com should not be for Christians, because we are to seek God for everything in our lives.

I recall attending one of our Pentecostal Assemblies of the World annual conventions in 2007 in Nashville, TN. A well-known bishop was preaching one evening, and after the mass choir finished singing its last song, he got up to prepare the delivery of his message. But before he gave the scripture and text, he was promoting his new book by giving out free copies to some of the saints in the congregation. Then he said, "There are just too many single saints within the body of Christ, so I have a partnership with this website for Christian people to meet called Faithmate.com." Then why is he single?

Upon my return, I logged on to the site and created a profile. I attached a profile picture of myself in a classy Navy-blue first-lady hat, a navy blue and white two-piece suit that was neatly pressed, and my happy-to-see-you smile on my face.

I shared some of my skills. My highest education at that time was a bachelor's degree in business. When I replied to a question about what I was looking for in a man, I recall writing "a man who is saved and baptized in Jesus, filled with the Holy Ghost and determined to live for Jesus, a man who is living a holy and righteous life, and a man who will live right so he can die right in Christ." Then I hit the save button.

I began searching the website, reviewing some of the men's profiles. This was a mistake. I almost fell out my chair when I saw the profiles. Some of them said things like, "I occasionally drink," or "I occasionally smoke," or "I occasionally party…but I am looking for a good Christian woman."

What? Really? I wondered, "Do they know Christian means Christ-like? What in the world is going on here? These men were looking for a good Christian woman, and they were not good Christian men.

I recall e-mailing one man to ask him what he was doing on a Christian site looking for a woman when he was still married. His profile stated that he was separated from his wife. He emailed me back, very angry, and said he was just looking for someone to talk to. I replied, "Talk to Jesus."

I believe Christian, saved women should not be looking for saved men on these so-called Christian websites. We should not pursue men. The Bible is clear and straight to the point.

Proverbs 18:22 — *Whoso findeth a wife, findeth a good thing and obtaineth favor of the Lord.*

The men are to pursue us. They are to come after the women, not the other way around. Do not get me wrong or twisted, I love relationships, because love makes all the difference when we have that special person to share with.

Love is honest. Love is not selfish. Love is truth. Love makes sacrifices, and love is also hope. While loving a person, there will be times when there will be intense fellowship, otherwise known as arguments or disagreements. This will allow people to get to know their mates better. If a man loves his wife as Christ does the church, that marriage will become awesome, and a couple as such would be able to help others with their marriages by sharing suggestions.

I love to love others; I am excited about the love that Jesus had for us when He gave His life on the cross so we may have eternal life. God's love is unconditional, as should our love be for our mate. I love sharing and giving love back! Love makes me smile; it makes me happy. Love is priceless!

We must be mindful of God's love for us as we ask the Lord to help us love ourselves. Be encouraged while asking the Lord to help us to become virtuous women, as in Proverbs 31:30: "Favor is deceitful, and beauty is vain; but a woman that feareth the Lord, she shall be praised."

Trusting God to provide a mate

I believe God has already divinely ordained a particular man or woman for us. If you recall the previous testimony of one of the Sunday school teachers in my church, God does not make mistakes. There are many biblical examples of God bringing couples together. These couple stayed together until death. In **Genesis 1:1–31**, God put Adam and Eve together. In **Genesis 6:1–22**, He put Noah and his wife together, as well as in St. **Matthew 1:18–21,** He also put Mary and Joseph together.

Now perhaps someone marriage is not working because that man or woman is not who God had for us in the first place. Because we disobeyed the plan and direction God had for us by selecting someone on our own, the Lord has to heal us, cleanse us, and prepare us for that man or woman He has intended for us to marry since the beginning of time. It sometimes takes a long time for the Lord to restore us because of the damage done in our previous relationships. The Lord has to help us trust again because of a cheating or abusive mate. The Lord has to heal those wounds from the past so that we are ready for our future.

Dating sites can be trouble

Perhaps the marriage is not working because you caught your saved husband on some of those dating websites. Well, if you caught your mate on a dating website, ask him or her why they were on the site in the first place? Begin to pray with each other and bind the hand of the enemy who is trying to destroy your marriage. Seek Godly counseling from the Elders of your church, if that is God's will for you and your mate. Keep your friends and family out of your marriage unless God tells you to share your story as a testimony.

If there is infidelity

Perhaps your marriage is not working because your saved, preaching husband has you as well as a little sweetheart from another church on the side. Perhaps he has both at a Christian convention, in the same hotel, but on different floors. If you have proof that your husband is cheating, pray and ask God what you should do. I say pray first, because if you do know with assurance that your spouse is cheating and you know who your husband's sweetheart is, you may feel like beating her down. God does not want the saints fighting each other. Pray and pray hard! Cry out for some help from the Lord!

As you pray, sit down and communicate with your mate. Sometimes greed and selfishness will motivate your mate to cheat. Saved men and women are human, too. Saints have the responsibility to push as hard as we can to do that which is pleasing to the Lord! It is very clear that cheating is not pleasing to Christ. We have to get to a place in God where we stop making excuses for sin. Jesus hates sin, and so should we. It is also very hard for a marriage to bounce back from infidelity because the trust needs to be regained. If you want to save your marriage, you need God to help both parties.

Trying a different approach

Perhaps your marriage is not working because you are trying to punish your mate by withholding sex.

Christian sisters, please stop trying to punish your husbands by withholding sex because you are mad. That is not the answer, because, although he is saved, the flesh is weak, and he may very well go to get some loving from someone else. Communicate with your mate, and tell him why you are angry. Let him know that what he did really hurt you. If you pray and change your approach, perhaps making up will cause sparks to begin flying and toes to wiggle. Instead, start by saying, “Honey, I love you,” instead of punishing him by withholding sex.

If you are married to a man or woman that God did not give you, this does not mean that your marriage can or will not work out! It may take a lot of hard work on both parts, but God is able to forgive you for stepping out of His plan for your life and place you in the direction that you should go. Begin praying with and for each other.

In my opinion, I believe dating websites are not God’s righteousness! Be encouraged to wait on the Lord for everything, every need, and every desire in your life. Remember, my Christian sisters and my Christian brothers, you matter to God!

Chapter 5 – Reality Hits After the Wedding

I never cooked for Chris when we were dating, so he was unaware that there were some foods that I was unable to prepare, but instead, he assumed that I could cook anything. Reality hit one day when I cooked steak for myself and the girls, and he wanted me to prepare fresh fish because he did not eat most meat. I was not used to cooking fresh fish, so I threw some fish sticks in the oven along with some tater tots. Chris' facial expression was priceless. I laughed very hard as he asked, "What is this?" Chris did not find the situation amusing, though. As time went on, I eventually learned how to prepare different types of fresh fish, such as salmon, flounder, and tilapia. I even learned how to prepare some delicious salmon cakes.

I eventually learned how to cook healthier meals, and I no longer had to prepare two separate meals, because fresh fish was good for everyone! It makes me laugh each time I recall this particular moment.

If you are dating the man or woman that God has given you, it may not be a bad idea to prepare a meal for that person while you are in the dating stage, just in case you need to brush up on your cooking skills. There is a saying, "The way to a man's heart is through his stomach." I am not sure how true this statement may be, but most men love to eat.

My Christian brothers and sisters, make sure you decide who, between the two of you, will be better at preparing the family meals. It is good if both of you are good at cooking. Ladies, if you cannot cook, it may be a good idea to get a few cookbooks or pull some recipes from the Internet and start practicing before getting married. Gentlemen, there is also nothing wrong if you decide to do all the cooking while your wife is doing all the cleaning. Make sure the communication is clear. Clarity should be established regarding who will do which chore.

Another serious reality issue that is rarely discussed when dating is finances. Neither Chris nor I were good at managing money. You should decide whether there will be a savings and checking account for the household budget as well as each mate having separate savings and checking accounts. I did not work for six months after giving birth to our daughter Octavia. Chris initially did well managing the bills and paying tithes and offerings, but after a while, things went wrong. Groceries got low, our phone was turned off for nonpayment, and our auto insurance lapsed. I started wondering what in the world was going on, so I decided to investigate. What I discovered was Chris stopped paying tithes and offerings in church, and this was not good! We could not put our giving on the back burner and expect our finances to flow smoothly. God loves a cheerful giver!

Then, Chris took money from the household to start his own business selling personal alarm systems. This lasted for two months, and then he ended with no sales and a big box of alarms that were tossed into the coat closet.

The lesson is not to start a business without discussing details with your wife or husband. Chris was determined to believe that he had the skills to sell these personal alarms. I did not support him because he had already made his mind up before discussing it with me. First of all, an entrepreneur must be energetic and business-minded. Second an entrepreneur cannot and should not be lazy. Another lesson was to avoid these pyramid-type scams. Investigate the company to see if it is real. If you have to recruit people under you before there is a profit, then say no. Pay close attention to the upfront investment. Ask a consultant if a website can be created for your customers to purchase items being sold. Find out if there are reviews of this company online. Be very careful of the many other scams that can rip you off when trying to begin your own business. Know that money issues can destroy a marriage!

Husbands and wives, try communicating. Allow the one who is more responsible to manage the household finances. In our case, one of us had to step up to the plate in managing the finances. Also, establish a household account for the family budget, as well as a separate account for activities and purchases that are outside of the family budget. On payday, pay the Lord first, and then pay yourselves a bi-weekly allowance. By establishing such a plan, you will avoid taking money from the bills and household expenses. It will prevent you from robbing Peter to pay Paul.

So after I became pregnant with Octavia, Chris and I decided that we would not have any more children. Three girls were going to be enough. Feeding and taking care of the girls was a lot of work, and Chris gave very little help. The responsibility of having to cook, do laundry, comb hair for three girls, and clean the house all fell on me. Chris just continued to flip the TV from channel to channel while wondering when dinner was going to be ready. Though I enjoyed being a wife and mom, I could not do it all!

When Octavia was born, the doctor told me to wait six weeks, then come back to get my tubes tied, but when I did, the doctor said she could not do it.

"Why?" I asked.

"You are six weeks pregnant," she replied.

I was stunned. I asked her to repeat herself. She did. Chris decided to have a vasectomy instead.

We found out that we were having a boy. I was excited after about the fifth month of pregnancy. Christopher Jr. was born eleven months after Octavia. It was like having twins. Preparing bottles for both was stressful. I put formula in one bottle and whole milk in the other, until one day I got them mixed up. When that happened, I started giving Octavia sippy cups instead of a bottle.

My hands were full. I began to feel sad and unattractive after taking such good care of the family with nobody to take care of me. I was married, but feeling like a single parent. I wondered to myself if Chris had lost interest in me, when in fact the interest was never there. He was not trying to give me the intimate time couples needed. All he wanted was his breakfast, lunch, and dinner, a clean house, and clean uniforms for work.

We, as mothers, do not start families by ourselves, and we should not have to carry the load ourselves. Husbands and wives must work together with balancing the family, church, work, and activities. Wives and moms, you must be careful not to lose yourself while taking care of your family. Find an hour or two for you to do something relaxing. Then set some time aside for you and your husband. It is important to create balance while being fruitful and multiplying.

Husbands, do not neglect your wives. Tell her how special she is to you. Let your wife know that even after four children, she still looks beautiful. Let your wife know often how much you love her. Spend those intimate moments with her without the children being present.

Wives, do not stop taking care of your appearances after having your children. Keep yourselves looking and smelling good! Let your husband know that you appreciate all he does for the family. This applies to the couples who are working as a team to keep balance within the family. If, in fact, you are unable to work together, it may not be a bad idea to pray together for guidance from the Lord. Times like these are when you both can pray for each other. You can pray with each other, whether your mate is from the Lord or yourself. I am not saying that just because you are not with the person who God has selected for you that things cannot work out, because things can; however it may take extra work. Christian couples should be in the habit of taking everything to God in prayer.

There are many examples of couples whose Christian mates did not come from the Lord and things are working out. As an example, a close family member told me that God did not put them together, but they have learned how to work through the hard times by praying instead of calling it quits. It is very important to keep the romance and spark alive within your marriage by setting time aside for the intimacy, doing things like taking hot showers together, having candle-light dinners, or cuddling up together to watch a good movie while eating a bowl of hot, buttered popcorn. It is okay to do these things as a couple. I do not believe you will go to hell for spicing up your marriage. Enjoy each other, because, after all, you are married!

Chapter 6 – Trust

Proverbs 3:5–7 — *Trust in the Lord with all thy heart; and lean not unto thine own understanding. In all thy ways acknowledge him, and he shall direct thy paths. Be not wise in thy own eyes; fear the Lord and depart from evil.*

Know with assurance that the Christian person you are dating is who God has designed for you to marry. As you place your complete trust in the Lord, make sure you trust one another.

I do not believe Chris was the person who the Lord designed for me to marry, and as a result of marrying him, I stepped completely out of God's will and plan for my life. I chose to marry Chris on my own! Our trust in each other died when Chris' pager went off and I asked who was paging him this late at night. Chris replied with, "It's just a friend." Was it really just a friend, or some woman on the side? I recall once when our house phone rang and I answered it. A female voice on the other end said, "Hello."

I said, "Hello."

She said, "My name is Jackie, is Chris available? Chris and I are old friends."

Now I was trying to figure out how and why this woman had our home number.

I said, "Well, this is Chris' wife."

Jackie said, "Oh, hi. I heard a lot about you."

I said, "Funny, because I have not heard anything about you."

I later found out this was a woman that Chris was once engaged to while he was on active duty. I handed Chris the phone and sat in the living room boiling like a pot of hot water for some creamy grits! They talked for about an hour.

Once their conversation was over and Chris hung up the phone, I said, "Chris, you never mentioned anything about Jackie to me during our dating period."

Chris said, "Oh, well, she is someone I dated while in the military."

I asked, "Why is she calling our house?"

Chris said, "I thought maybe you and Jackie could become friends."

I said, "Chris, are you out of your devil mind? Are you high?"

Chris then said, "I do not think there is anything wrong with you two becoming friends."

I began to yell, "Are you kidding me? I am not interested in becoming friends with someone you used to be sexually involved with!"

Situations such as this can destroy trust. Even with the person that God has blessed you with to marry, both parties must pray daily. The devil will bring back those old girlfriends or boyfriends. The devil will bring back all those old memories.

There are many cheating spouses within the church!

Chris and I sat down to discuss Jackie's call. I was angry that he never mentioned her to me. I was wondering how long Jackie and Chris had been talking for her to have our home number. I told Chris that he should not be speaking with Jackie because they were not just sexually involved—they were once engaged.

Chris replied, "Why can't I be friends with Jackie? Says who? Who makes these rules for married people?"

I said, "Chris, it is just not about rules, but it is about respect for the marriage and for each other!"

Other women should not talk to your husband more than you do! Leave the exes alone and move on. Allow your spouse to become your best friend. Obey the Word of God regarding every man having his own wife. This is singular, not plural! No marriage is perfect! We have the devil against us. We may have in-laws against us. We have ex-friends against us. What can become complicated may also become a crisis. It is important for a couple to be on the same page.

After our argument, Chris' behavior changed dramatically. He would say, "Honey, I am going out to the store."

I would say, "This time of night?"

Chris would say "Yes, Wal-Mart is still open." Then he would take a shower, get dressed, and head out the door.

Ladies, we were not born last night. Who takes a shower at nine-o'clock at night to go to the store? He would return five hours later. Where was the store, in Georgia? Trust in our marriage was gone!

Beware of those who use *honey, I have to work late* a little too often, because it is the number one excuse for cheating! One example is when you receive a phone call stating, "Honey, do not wait up for me tonight," then your spouse comes home at two or three o'clock in the morning smelling like cheap cologne or perfume. Another example is some pastors, doctors, lawyers, or police officers who often work long hours and may say they have to work late, then later you find out they are dating a co-worker or secretary and, once again, they are coming home at two or three o'clock the next morning. Professions such as these are the perfect cover-ups for cheating and will destroy the trust in a marriage.

Lack of trust can become an issue for someone who was once married but is now divorced as a result of infidelity that occurred during the marriage. A situation such as this is very difficult because there could be many unresolved issues on so many levels. Possibly, no real closure has taken place. Unresolved issues may occur due to guilt, unforgiveness, or shame from either party involved—or both. It becomes even more difficult in a situation where the former spouse has died, but there was no closure for the surviving ex-spouse prior to the death.

Perhaps this wasn't the person God divinely created for us, and now our ex-spouse has divorced us, remarried, and had kids with their new partner, leaving us devastated and hurt. And now, this person had the nerve to die on us! Yes, it is very easy for us to carry guilt and shame. But we must forgive ourselves so we can become emotionally complete with this part of our lives.

Is there a way to obtain complete closure of the relationship which ended in divorce? Can one move on to a new relationship carrying the guilt of the past? We have to learn to ask God to help us with the guilt from our past! Holding on to the guilt from our past can prevent us from moving forward in our future with the person God has ordained for us. We become hard on ourselves, making it difficult to let go! We are also ashamed of the failing of the relationship, marriage, and friendship and may not want to go through it again.

Writing can be very therapeutic; maybe writing a goodbye letter to an ex-mate letting the person know how you feel regarding the marriage, how you allowed it to fail, and how the way things ended has impacted your life since the divorce. Writing this type of letter can be healing for the heart. Continue with prayer, asking God to help you to forgive this person for your own peace of mind so you can see the bigger purpose.

Also, a woman serving the Lord who is a single parent but has the desire to marry or remarry must encourage herself to seek and wait on the Lord. There are many benefits to waiting on God. First of all, the Lord knows not just who will be the best husband to us, but He also knows who will be the best father to our child or children.

Things happen within the church that should not happen to women and children. Sometimes men know they can get a good woman from church, and some even prey on those who are single parents, perhaps just to get close to that single parent's child. Second of all, God will give you discernment when that man or woman is not good for you or your children, because He only desires the best for you! Yes, the Lord has given us free will, as stated before, but delighting yourself in Him is finding great pleasure in Jesus and committing your ways unto Him while trusting the Lord to have your back! We must truly be led by God according to the scriptures. Pastoral counseling is critical to anyone considering marriage and will prevent you from ignoring very obvious biblical principles required by all to be successfully married. The challenge is that God will not force Himself on us. Sometimes we become so driven with emotions, lust, and personal motives that we forget about being observant of the spiritual lifestyle of the person we are interested in or may already be dating. Prayer and spiritual counseling are essential to not confuse God's will with your own heart's desire. Remember Chapter Two on "Dating": choose to follow those steps and do not ignore God's warning signs. The world or unsaved may say, **"You make your own rules."**

Family, friends, and church folks seem to have opinions about and advice for single mothers and their private lives. But it is best to wait on God! Though your past may be very hurtful and hard to let go, there is purpose for your pain.

We must become completely and totally free from our past. We speak freedom from this day forward, in Jesus' name!

CB

Chapter 7 – Infidelity

There may be many Christian sisters and brothers who are hurting due to infidelity that happened in their marriage right within the church. Regardless of what your husband or wife may be doing, there is never an excuse or reason for cheating!

Unresolved childhood issues may be a factor that leads to infidelity. If a person has unresolved issues within their relationship or marriage, then they will have a difficult time with anyone being good for them. For example, if a person is struggling to commit to the person they are dating or married to, then this person may be dealing with commitment issues from their childhood. If they are struggling with being faithful and continue to abandon the relationship, then perhaps they are dealing with their parents' unfaithfulness, or maybe one of their parents abandoned the entire family.

Infidelity is extremely hard for a couple to bounce back from, because trust has been lost. With a lot of hard work, prayer, and determination from both mates, it can restored, but both have to be willing to forgive and be forgiven. Keep in mind that lies and secrets are like mold growing in the basement walls of a house. The mold can be an expensive price to pay and an expensive repair.

If you are counseling single Christians through your ministry, perhaps it would be better for a husband and wife counsel as a team. This allows the good work of counseling to remain genuine, and will allow the husband-and-wife team to avoid temptation. Not everyone in church is there to serve and live for the Lord. Anyone who is not in church for Jesus can very well be in place to destroy a marriage by flirting with your wife or your husband. Even if you are with the woman or man that God has given you to marry, never underestimate the tricks of the devil.

Words of Encouragement:
Stay focused as a couple, stay prayerful, and stay attentive to each other.

Each time I sensed Chris cheating, I would confront him about it. I was never wrong. He would admit it. This let me know that he was not going to stop committing adultery. Although I walked around with so much hurt on the inside, I continued to focus on my children, church, and school work.

Chris accused me of having an affair, as well. The look on my face was the same as a child caught with their hands in the cookie jar, like when I was growing up and mom said we could not have any cookies until after dinner.

I asked, "What do you mean I was having an affair, too?"

He said, "You were having an affair with the church."

I laughed until I had tears falling, but I understood what Chris was saying. Although there was no reason for Chris to cheat, we as saints of God must have balance when managing family, work, and church.

We can become married to the church when we participate in various ministries that cause us to begin neglecting our family. Chris would often come home to dinner that I prepared and left on the stove while the children and I were at church, leaving him to eat dinner alone. This contributed to Chris' frustrations. He wanted to keep me home cooking, cleaning, and attending to him, but I felt, due to the neglect I was receiving from Chris, that the children and church were all that mattered.

I have learned from a biblical leadership class that we should not be on more than two ministries because we cannot give one hundred percent if we are on three or more ministries. If we are at church seven days a week, how can we take care of home? We can go completely overboard with becoming busy and still not be doing what God wants us to do!

Husbands and wives cheat for many reasons. In our case, it was due to greed and selfishness on Chris' part, and perhaps this is the reason things fell apart. It was clear that the situation with our marriage was going to require many compromises to find a balance between family, work, and church.

Having the mate God has designed for us is not so we can put Him on the back burner while we attend to everything it requires to care for our mates. We cannot stay in church around the clock and neglect our mates, but on the other hand, we also cannot make our mates the gods of our lives. We have to ask God for balance and leave no space for the enemy.

I recall watching a show called "Unfaithfulness." It was about a couple with no children who had not been married long. The wife went on travel, leaving her husband home alone. After a few days, the wife connected with someone she met on travel and had sex with this person. Back at home, the husband called up an old girlfriend and invited her over, and they began having sex. Afterwards, he told his old girlfriend that he was married and what they just did can never happen again.

The wife returned home after two weeks, and her husband noticed something different. Now both of them were keeping a secret, but the wife got caught first by speaking with the guy on her cell phone. Her husband heard the conversation and made her call the guy back so he could speak with him. The guy stated that they were just friends, but the husband knew they had slept together. The next few weeks were intense, but then the husband could no longer deal with the guilt he was feeling and confessed to his wife that he invited his old girlfriend over to have sex with her in the couple's home. The couple decided to go to counseling and work through this issue. They completed counseling and decided to forgive each other and have been married for six years since the infidelity.

Some husbands and wives are not happy with the intimacy with their spouses. Some are neglected emotionally and sexually; however, there is never an excuse for cheating.

I Corinthians 7:3 — *Let the husband render unto the wife due benevolence; and likewise also the wife unto the husband.*

Couples meet and get married at a very young ages all the time; it is not uncommon. When it comes to married couples who are in the church, sometimes each has their individual career and ministry working within their church. After being married a really long time, it sometimes happens that one mate commits adultery due to their career, schedule, and the limited time that they have to spend with each their partner. One case that I am familiar with is a well-known child of God who committed a terrible act by sleeping with their friend's mate, and it destroyed their family. The excuse given was that it happened because the mate was always on the road traveling, promoting and building their ministry, and did not spend enough time with their spouse. Both parties were very devastated and began to encourage married couples to make time for each other.

It is my belief that many people have taken the Scripture in Genesis out of context that says God created Adam in His own image said it was not good for man to be alone! Today, this statement has gone to another level, because there is so much cheating going on within the church. It's not good that man should be alone, but each man is to have only one wife, not a wife and a sweetheart on the side! It is not good for a woman to be alone either, but we are not the pursuers; we are created to be the helpmate to the partner God has created for us. We should be encouraged to stop coming to church looking for husbands and instead focus on seeking the Kingdom of God!

Although I was not receiving love, romance, attention, and intimacy from my husband, and I was married but yet single, it would have been very wrong for me to find a sugar daddy on the side. That would not have been pleasing to the Lord!

Husbands and wives should not hold out on one another. My husband would sometimes allow months to pass before spending intimate time with me, even while he had affairs. When he decided to leave because he no longer wanted the marriage, I did not stop him, but I said "hallelujah!"

If you would like to save your marriage, even when it is not the person God ordained for you to marry, I encourage you to seek help now. Make sure both of you want the same things in order to repair your marriage. Hold on to the love you have for God and each other.

Once infidelity has taken place within a marriage, it is very hard to bounce back without some form of counseling and much prayer! Some people make excuses for a husband, or wife who has cheated, but such an act is very displeasing to God.

When a husband or wife decides they are going to cheat, it starts with a thought first. You are given a chance to rebuke that thought and not act on it. Often times, it is not that the needs are not being met at home, but plain disobedience to the Word of God. It is plain sin. If, in fact, your needs are not being met and you are being emotionally and sexually neglected, I encourage prayer for your wife or husband. Give the situation to God! Trust and believe that the Lord will work things out! Communicate with your spouse about your feelings. Seek Godly counseling, which can be counseling with your pastor or spiritual mentor, because they will give you some scriptures to stand on while seeking the Lord for a solution. Seeking Godly counseling is not a bad thing. Most often, your spiritual leader or pastor has experienced what you are now going through with your needs being neglected if it is God's will to go that route. It was His will for me to seek counseling for my own peace of mind, but Jesus is the best counselor because the Word says so!

> **Isaiah 9:6** — *For unto us a child is born, unto us a son is given: and the government shall be upon his shoulder, and his name shall be called Wonderful*

Counselor, The mighty God, The everlasting Father, The Prince of Peace.

If your wife or husband is struggling with pornography, I also encourage much prayer. Pray with your spouse. Pray for your spouse. Pray that your spouse is delivered from the dysfunctions that may have caused the perversion. Communicate how you are feeling about the pornography. It would not be wise to turn a blind eye. And again, seek Godly counseling.

God wants us be free from all past hurts!
God wants us to be free from all past pain!
God wants us to be free from all past abuse!

After God delivers us from damage caused by stepping out of His will for our lives, then and only then are we ready for the mate He has divinely created for us!

Perhaps you are praying with and for your spouse and you feel that prayer is not enough; however, I cannot imagine prayer not being enough, because that is what got me through all of my hurt, pain, and disappointments. I am reminded of a song:

Don't stop praying, for the Lord is nigh,
Don't stop praying, He will hear your cry,
For the Lord has promised, and His Word is true,
Don't stop praying, He will answer you.

If prayer is not working, be encouraged to try a marriage retreat, a marriage counselor for some therapy exercises, or role play your issues out. I still cannot imagine prayer not working, but perhaps this is not the person you were to marry. I encourage you to really work hard to keep your marriage, because it becomes hard when marriages break up. It is not just hard on the couple, but it is very hard on the children.

I recall after my husband left us, my son cried for a while because he wanted his daddy. My heart was so heavy because our home had been broken. Each time my husband would pick up our children to spend a day with him, upon their return, our son would cry for hours until he would fall to sleep. Then six months after my husband left, we became homeless, which added to the pain. As we began the divorce process, Chris and I were to alternate every other holiday and weekend with the children. This meant the children were being exposed to two different lifestyles.

I believe a divorce is much harder on the children. They go through emotional and mental trauma. No child should have to experience a broken home.

Try to make your marriage work.

CB

Chapter 8 – Delivered and Set Free

I struggled with fornication for many years after rededicating my life to Christ, which was after having my second child out of wedlock. During my struggle, I would always talk to the Lord and reread **Acts 15:28–29** "*For it seemed good to the Holy Ghost, and to us, to lay upon you no greater burden than these necessary things; that ye abstain from meats offered to idols, and from blood, and from things strangled, and from fornication: from which if ye keep yourselves, ye shall do well. Fare ye well.*"

This chapter was Paul and Barnabas teaching the apostles and the people about great concerns that they were having regarding circumcision. This meant to me a form of cleanliness, and if I continued in fornication, I was not clean. I also often felt sad for disappointing the Lord. Now, does this mean I wasn't saved? Some within the body of Christ would say yes, but because I had a heart to do right, I knew eventually I would reach my deliverance. Also, **Ephesians 5:1–3** says: "Be ye therefore followers of God, as dear children. And walk in love, as Christ also hath loved us, and hath given himself for us an offering and a sacrifice to God for a sweet-smelling Savior. But fornication, and all uncleanness, or covetousness, let it not be once named among you, as becometh saints."

After reading Paul's teachings, I wanted to develop such a life style that would put a smile on God's face! I did not want to do good for six months or so, and then fall into fornication again and disappoint the Lord. Each time I would fall into sin, participating in what I call **a revolving door**, it became harder and harder to get out of this never-changing routine, so I thought, because the flesh became weaker and weaker. The mind and heart were saying NO, but my flesh at times got the best of me. Why was that? Why did my flesh win? Because I became slack in my prayer life and studying God's Word, therefore I had nothing to fight the temptation. Now staying free and delivered is a mission of mine. I make sure that I pray daily with a mind to obey the Word and will of God. If we do not pray and study to show ourselves approved unto God, which is our responsibility, we are going to fail. It is a wonderful blessing now to be able to worship and praise the Lord without being bound by sin. The freedom I have is priceless, but I cannot get comfortable and slack in my prayer life, and I must stay in the Word of God. We must push forward to avoid practicing sin.

If we, as saints, do not fast, pray, and force ourselves to apply the Word of God to our lives, it will be like a revolving door. What I mean by that is we have to change our focus on the fact that we are single and focus more on our purpose in Christ. While focusing on our purpose, we must remain dedicated to the Word of God by studying daily and then applying it to our lives.

My mind goes back to when Jesus was walking on the water and He bid Peter to come. Peter did well walking on the water until he took his eyes off Jesus, and then at that moment, Peter began to sink. Well, it is the same thing when it comes to our struggles with sin and fornication. If we take our eyes off Jesus and what He has for us to do, we will sink right back into sin.

Even in ministry, we must remain focused and not become weary in well-doing, because it only takes a second to fall. It is the enemy's job to set traps for us. Those traps can be in or out of the church, but the key is to stay focused so we can stay free!

CB

Chapter 9 – The Power to Let Go

We have the power within us to let go of all past hurt, pain, disappointment, devastations, and relationships. We have to ask "Can I let this go?" The answer is yes! If we are willing to confront and not cover up the emotions associated with the toxic relationship, then yes, we can let go.

Now, there are several reasons we have difficulty letting go in order to move forward.

One reason is guilt, even though it may not be completely our fault that we feel guilty for how we responded to the situations which occurred within the relationship.

The second reason we have difficulty letting go is unforgiveness. We may not be willing to forgive the person who has wronged us during the course of the marriage or relationship. We may feel that the person has robbed us of true happiness, that fairytale dream, and even sex because of committing adultery. The third reason is because of anger. We may be angry in response to how we are being treated within the relationship or marriage. Anger will cause us to remain stuck because of the unwillingness to work the situation out with each other. We may want our mate to feel the exact same pain they are causing us to feel. The last reason, but not least, is denial. We can be in denial that a problem even exists. We can be in denial that this is the wrong person for us. We can even be in denial that the marriage or relationship is ending because of not wanting to face reality, so we begin to make excuses. After all, who gets married only to find themselves getting a divorce? The fact of the matter is we must let go by living in the present. What I mean by that is by focusing on our ministry in Christ and building up our prayer life while confronting the emotions associated with the issues within the marriage or relationship. Letting go is for our own peace of mind and it will prevent us from becoming bitter and stuck.

To the woman who by nature is born and ready to be swept off her feet by a prince charming, who wants to start a family after having her dream wedding, and live happily ever-after. Well, know that it is okay to desire to be married, but remember the importance having the person who is right for you according to God. It is natural that we are to marry and be fruitful and multiply. But remember, timing is everything, so with that being said, be encouraged by waiting and praying to hear directly from the Lord, Who knows who and what is best for you. While waiting, remain engaged in knowing your purpose in Christ and by knowing your gifts and talents. Become involved in your community by mentoring young teens or assisting seniors.

We can fight the weakness of our flesh by crucifying the flesh daily through fasting, praying, and building God an altar wherever we are. **Romans 8:4-6**: *That the righteousness of the law might be fulfilled in us, who walk not after the flesh, but after the Spirit. For they that are after the flesh do mind the things of the flesh; but they that are after the Spirit the things of the Spirit. For to be carnally minded is death; but to be spiritually minded is life and peace.* We can put a smile on Jesus' face by staying focused and by not practicing sin! Satan will continue to try and set us up to fail God, but we do not have to fail. We do have a responsibility to live by the Word of God! Each time we do not trust God to keep us until we are married, we are settling for whoever comes our way.

Many young women have allowed themselves to become stuck in relationships for many years just to say they have a man, but wonder why this man will not marry them. It is crazy to live in such a mess. We don't have to. Our lives matter to God! God only wants the best for us. If you have been in a relationship for two or three years and he has not popped that one question—"Will you marry me?"—then you may want to reassess the relationship. Go on a fast and pray for direction. We do not have to subject ourselves to less when God wants to give us life more abundantly!

Why are marriages not lasting within our churches? The divorce rate seems to be pretty high. Some of the reasons are the same reasons for why the divorce rate is so high in the world, which include:

- Abuse
- Domestic violence
- Finances
- Substance abuse by the unsaved spouse
- Infidelity
- Lack of commitment
- Extramarital affairs

And the list goes on and on. We may be surprised, but these issues do take place right in churches.

How do we begin to promote healthy relationships? We promote healthy relationships with our mate by becoming true to God, true to ourselves, and true to our mates.

CB

Chapter 10 – Step-Parenting

Before my husband and I married, I was a single parent of two children. During our pre-counseling sessions, the pastor warned him that he was entering into an already made family. He mentioned to Chris that he would have to be willing to accept the fact that my daughters might never see him as their dad, but as Mr. Chris.

Step parenting is rarely easy, therefore, if you are dating someone who already has children from previous relationships, ask yourself, "Am I ready to become a stepparent?"

My husband and I should have been on the same page when it came to the children, but we were not. He would often favor one daughter more than the other, and I believed in fairness with both girls. When parents are not on the same page, the children will sense it and play one parent against the other. Chris found step parenting to be a challenge, although he grew up with a stepfather. We eventually learned the importance of working together as a team by keeping the lines of communication open regarding the children and what they were allowed to participate in.

~Blended Family~

Blended families can derive from remarriage, adoption, and biological parents reappearing in a child's life.

Essential information for my husband becoming my daughters' stepfather was not discussed in detail. My husband and I did not realize at that time how important it was to establish those essential details, such as who would be the disciplinarian, or which one of us would decide where they could go and what they could do. The girls expressed dissatisfaction at first because they were not ready to share me, their mom. My husband also could not have me without accepting the girls.

A dissatisfied stepchild will cause turmoil and chaos within the household. It is very important to form strategies before becoming a blended family by communicating ideas that will help build the relationship between the children and the stepparent. It sometimes can take years to build the necessary love and bond between the children and stepparent, especially if the biological parents are still involved in the child's life.

Although Chris had nieces and nephews, he was new to the role of parenting. It was not clear or discussed where he fit and where his responsibilities lay. Sometimes, with step parenting, the bond between the child and stepmom or stepdad can be special and unique, and sometimes not. In our case, it was not!

I encourage stepparents to work together with the biological parents in building a good relationship with the children. Be clear regarding consequences and rules, which are areas where my husband and I differed. My husband believed in beating or whipping a child for every little thing, but I believed in allowing a child to be a child and that the punishment must fit the crime.

With the two youngest children that we had together, we had a total of four children. Chris was not just a stepdad, but a biological dad to his only two children. My hands were full as a mom of four children. My husband felt the little time he was giving to me was being taken away because of my duties to the children. Jealousy set in because he felt he deserved all of my attention on his terms. Perhaps if he helped with the chores and the children, there would have been more time to repair and work on our marriage.

Our two youngest children paid close attention to everything going on within the home. Octavia would ask more questions than Chris Jr. She would ask questions such as why her last name was different than her sisters. She asked why daddy was so mean to me. I asked her why she thought her dad was mean to me, and she said, "Because daddy never goes anywhere with us." She then said, "Mommy, if my husband treats me like daddy treats you, I am putting him on time out!" I laughed so hard. Then she said, "That is what you should have done before you married daddy." I thought to myself, this little girl is speaking as an old, wise person.

Children are very observant. We, as parents and stepparents, may not think these kids are paying attention until we are holding a conversation with them; then you realize how important it is to lead by example. I found myself explaining to Octavia about her sisters' dad—that they all shared the same mom, but only she and CJ had the same dad. Octavia was a deep kid!

Prayer will help parents and stepparents face the truth about every area of the blended family and the many obstacles that will arise. Prayer will help parents, stepparents, and the children face the truth about the emotions that will destroy a marriage, such as, jealousy, hate, guilt, and resentment.

If I had stayed on the plan that God had for my life, this conversation with Octavia would not have been necessary. All of this took place because of my complete disobedience to God's will and resulted from my own self-inflicted trials. I married someone who perhaps might have had a hidden agenda and might not really have loved me the way Christ loves the church. People who do not love themselves are incapable of loving anyone else.

Chapter 11 – God's Plan

Genesis 1:27 *— So God created man in his own image, in the image of God created he him; male and female. And God blessed them, and God said unto them, be fruitful and multiply, and replenish the earth.*

My Christian sisters and brothers, this is where it all began. Adam and Eve had the first marriage. Paul was speaking to the church in Corinth regarding marriage. This is the difference, or should be the difference, between saved couples' dating until they are married and the unsaved couples' dating system.

I Corinthians 7:2–3 *— Nevertheless to avoid fornication, let every man have his own wife and let every woman have her own husband. Let the husband render unto the wife due benevolence and likewise also the wife unto the husband.*

In our society today, there are more and more couples shacking for many years and never getting married. This is not what God wants for the saints. Pastors and preachers must continue to lead by example and preach against sin! They must teach against fornication, adultery, and everything that is against the Word of God. Leaders have a responsibility to do right with no excuses for practicing sin. All of the saints of God have a responsibility to do what God is calling us to do. Many saved couples have already had pre-marital sex by the time they walk down that aisle to marry, and sadly, the church has accepted this type of behavior, which is not pleasing to God.

> **Romans 12:1-2** — *I beseech you therefore, brethren, by the mercies of God, that ye present your bodies a living sacrifice, holy, acceptable unto God, which is your reasonable service. And be not conformed to this world; but be ye transformed by the renewing of your mind, that ye may prove what is that good, and acceptable, and perfect, will of God.*

When a person is fornicating, committing adultery, and everything that is displeasing to the Lord, it is not a mistake. Affairs should not be taking place within the church.

> ***I Corinthians 7:8–9*** — *I say, therefore to the unmarried and widows it is good for them if they abide even as I. But if they cannot contain, let them marry; for it is better to marry than to burn.*

There are some who do not ever want to become married. That is fine, but do not discourage those who would like to marry. If you are happy being single, make sure you live according to the Word of God. If you plan to remain single until Jesus returns, do not get caught with your pants down, living in sin. Do not get caught having sex outside of marriage while insisting you are enjoying your singleness in Jesus!

If the husband and wife were unsaved at the time of the marriage and then one of the spouses becomes saved, Paul said in **I Corinthians 7:14: "For the unbelieving husband is sanctified by the wife, and the unbelieving wife is sanctified by the husband."**

Do not feel like you need to divorce your wife or husband because they are not saved and living for the Lord. Continue to live a saved life in front of them. Pray for them and with them. Invite them out to church activities and encourage them to become involved. Ask the Lord for balance. Do not leave your spouse at home while you are in church every day of the week.

~Focus on Purpose~

St. Matthew 6:33 — *But seek ye first the Kingdom of God, and his righteousness; and all these things shall be added unto you.*

God must come first in our lives. All of us were born with a purpose in Christ, but many do not know what that purpose is yet. Once you are saved and filled with the Holy Spirit, a change takes place in your life.

Some of our habits, addictions, and issues were immediately gone upon accepting salvation and the newness in Christ. Some issues remained, which means we have work to do by killing the flesh daily. In order for us to become Christ like and stay Christ like, there is work to be done in us. It is work to be done through us. We have to pray harder. We have to study the Word of God longer. We must remain focused on God's plan for our lives in order for us not slip back into sin.

II Corinthians 5:17 — *Therefore if any man be in Christ, he is a new creature; old things are passed away; behold, all things become new.*

We are not perfect people, but we have to develop a desire to please the Lord by not practicing sin. We must get to a point in life where we stop making excuses for sinning. Yes, we all make mistakes. Let's be clear: Deliberately sinning or practicing sin is not a mistake, because you are willfully disobeying the Word of the Lord. It is very important for us as saints of God to stop making excuses for sin!

Sex outside of marriage is sin! Sex before marriage can be a set-up for failure on so many levels, including emotionally, physically, and spiritually. We should not justify sin! We should not pacify sin! It is not just the young Christian people, but the older Christians as well. How can adults, teachers, preachers, and parents teach our children to wait until they become married before becoming sexually active when we are single and sexually active within the church? It is important for us to lead by example.

There will be many tempting opportunities. That man will appear to be everything you may have dreamed of. That woman may appear to have all the qualities that you may desire. Even so, we must remain focused.

We may have someone enticing us to do wrong by sinning. If there is a sister or brother within your church or within someone else's church trying to get you to have sex by telling you that God understands and God knows that we are human, I encourage you to keep your distance from that particular individual. Anyone encouraging you to disobey the Word of God is not the man or woman God has for you. A person of that nature is a stumbling block for you to fail the Lord! With the help of the Lord, if we become determined to represent Jesus, then we are able to hold out until He blesses us to become married.

I recall a sister in church who had a beautiful voice and sang on the choir. One day, she told the Pastor that the Lord had called her to preach. Prior to her first sermon, she was very faithful to the church's prison ministry. Upon completing her ministerial classes and preaching her first sermon, she continued ministering in song with the choir as a lead soloist as well as ministering the Word of God to the inmates. A few years had gone by, and one Sunday morning, the Pastor announced her engagement to be married. About a year later she was married.

The Lord blessed the couple with a baby, and she took some time off from the choir. She then had another baby, and as her children began to grow up, we noticed she slowly stopped coming to church. She was no longer involved with the prison ministry or with the choir. Our assistant Pastor jokingly said to her that the honeymoon was over, so she could come back to church, but we stopped seeing her and the family in church. Come to find out, she and her family relocated to another state. We will never know if she was offended by the pastor's comment. Sadly, it seems that this is also one of the issues where churches can sometimes go wrong; instead of drawing people in, it sometimes causes them to be turned away, especially when it presents a conflict in terms of what they are and are not capable of doing. I do not believe the Lord blesses us with mates so that we give up on serving Him. Only the Lord can help us balance family and ministry. Though it is very important for us to take care of home and family, God is important as well. He does not want us to forsake our families, nor does He wants us to forsake ministry. This can become something that can be very difficult on a new marriage, and especially when young children also come into play, which requires a lot of attention and nurturing. Unfortunately, what we find is that man will sometimes place certain requirements on people that God is not necessarily requiring.

In Steve Harvey's book *Act Like a Lady, Think Like a Man*, some of his suggestions are based on society's way of dating. We are new creatures in Christ Jesus and have begun our new walk in him. It is very important for us to think like Jesus.

Philippians 2:5 — *Let this mind be in you, which was also in Christ Jesus.*

If we are thinking as Christ did, then we most definitely can act as Christ did. This is what our new life is all about.

How do we stay focused until the Lord blesses us with our mate?

First, we must develop a strong prayer life. I cannot stress this enough! Prayer is so essential to our spiritual growth. It is very important that we know what our true calling in life is by communicating with the Lord, and expressing our concerns, impossibilities, and questions to him for guidance and direction.

Second, we must study the Word of God as we hide the Word in our hearts. The Word will keep us on track and prevent us from allowing flesh to rule.

II Timothy 2:15 — *Study to shew thyself approved unto God, a workman that needeth not to be ashamed, rightly dividing the word of truth.*

Applying God's Word will guide us into our destiny. Will times get hard? Sure they will, but we must focus and live on our purpose. Know that our life is all about fulfilling the Will of Christ, trusting God that everything will balance out!

Let me share a short testimony. It is not over until God says it is over! There was a minister I was interested in dating and marrying. I knew him before he was saved, therefore I was so excited to see him serving the Lord. I prayed and spoke with the Lord regarding this person. I have not received an answer from the Lord yet, but I refuse to set myself up for failure. I continue to stay focused on my purpose regarding grief and loss outreach, as well as singing and traveling with my church choir. Yes, we have spoken over the phone and gone out to dinner and lunch, but it is so important for me to keep my distance at this time. Why? Because, once again, he may not be the man that the Lord has for me to marry. So I have to wait on the Lord, and continue seeking God's Will for my life.

We must believe and trust that the Lord knows who and what is best for us! Stay encouraged! Push to put a smile on God's face! Live by example. Lead by example. Be the example that God is looking for in these last days.

May God bless and keep you!

Say this prayer with me:

> *Dear Heavenly Father, thank you for loving us. Thank you for keeping us. Thank you for another opportunity. Thank you for another chance to get things right! Thank you for being who you are in our lives!*

Dear God, forgive us for our self-inflicted wounds, forgive us for all of our sins, known and unknown. Forgive us for stepping out of your will, Lord! Forgive us for not praying and seeking you before making decisions. Your Word lets us know that a good man's steps are ordered by you! I ask today and every day that you order our steps. Lead us. Guide us. Help us to walk in the direction you will have us to go!

We do not want to disappoint you, Jesus. You and only you know what is best for us. Make us whole. Make us clean. Set us free from all the things that may be keeping us bound. Lord, bless every single and married person within the Body of Christ. Touch and deliver those who are in an unhealthy relationship. Bless those who are engaged, that they keep you first in every area of their life. Bless and keep those that feel alone and help each person to know their own self-worth! Free us from all the mind games and misconceptions!

We are determined to please you, Lord. We are determined to put a smile on your face by walking in total and complete obedience. In Jesus' Name!

Appendix – Word Search Puzzles–
Just For Fun

God's Way

S	H	O	L	Y	B	C	D	P	E
A	C	S	I	N	G	L	E	U	M
L	H	H	J	L	O	V	E	R	A
V	U	F	P	E	D	G	H	P	R
A	R	I	U	J	S	K	L	O	R
T	C	M	R	S	P	U	T	S	I
I	H	N	R	O	L	I	S	E	A
O	P	U	Q	D	A	T	I	N	G
N	P	S	T	W	N	U	N	V	E
P	E	C	N	E	I	D	E	B	O
Q	Z	M	K	Y	S	L	V	X	A

1. Church
2. Dating
3. God's Plan
4. Holy
5. Jesus
6. Love
7. Marriage
8. Obedience
9. Purpose
10. Salvation
11. Single
12. Sin
13. Wait

Wrong Way

F	O	R	N	I	C	A	T	I	O	N
A	T	E	A	C	H	E	R	B	C	S
D	E	F	P	G	G	R	E	E	D	E
H	I	G	P	L	K	M	N	O	P	L
G	G	N	I	T	A	E	H	C	M	F
A	Q	R	M	G	R	Y	S	T	I	I
M	U	V	P	L	O	U	E	W	N	S
E	X	Y	E	Z	Y	L	D	R	I	H
S	K	D	R	S	Q	I	O	E	S	N
A	F	F	A	I	R	U	N	S	T	E
R	E	H	C	A	E	R	P	G	E	S
A	D	U	L	T	E	R	Y	W	R	S

1. **Adultery**
2. **Affair**
3. **Cheating**
4. **Fornication**
5. **Games**
6. **Greed**
7. **Gigolos**
8. **Lying**
9. **Minister**
10. **Player**
11. **Pimp**
12. **Preacher**
13. **Rude**
14. **Selfishness**
15. **Teacher**

Creating Time

C	A	B	D	C	Y	F	D	G	H	J	K
H	L	M	P	O	L	M	E	N	T	A	L
I	Q	R	D	M	L	S	C	S	T	U	Y
L	G	V	E	M	A	I	I	E	Y	E	L
D	N	D	D	U	U	N	S	C	D	M	I
R	I	L	N	N	X	T	I	I	U	O	M
E	L	O	E	I	E	I	O	O	T	T	A
N	E	H	L	C	S	M	N	H	S	I	F
W	S	E	B	A	L	A	N	C	E	O	X
Y	N	S	Z	T	R	C	U	V	L	N	W
X	U	U	P	I	M	Y	P	Q	B	S	R
L	O	O	T	O	V	Z	W	T	I	M	E
Y	C	H	U	R	C	H	U	X	B	H	L

1. Balance
2. Bible Study
3. Blended
4. Children
5. Church
6. Choices
7. Communication
8. Counseling
9. Decision
10. Emotions
11. Family
12. Household
13. Intimacy
14. Mental
15. Sexually
16. Time

About the Author

Towhanna A. Boston was born, reared, and educated in Philadelphia. Towhanna accepted Jesus Christ as her Lord and savior at age 17. She also completed 11 years in the Army. As a full-time mother of four wonderful children, Towhanna successfully completed her Bachelor of Science degree in Business Administration from Strayer University in Washington, D.C.

On September 11, 2004, Towhanna tragically lost her two youngest children, C.J., 7, and Tavi, 8, during an accident that resulted from a suspect who was fleeing police in Washington, D.C. Towhanna has found strength in her sorrow that has flourished into an encouraging voice to those who have suffered the excruciating pain of losing a loved one. St. Matthew 5:4 says: "Blessed are they that mourn, for they shall be comforted." Truly, nobody can comfort us like Jesus!

Towhanna believes that our tests and trials are not just for us, but so we can reach out and help others. She has since published a book titled *Hold to God's Unchanging Hands,* a story of faith, forgiveness, and victory. While writing *Hold to God's Unchanging Hands*, she was inspired to write a book titled *I Do, I Will, I Shouldn't Have*, on dating and marriage. Towhanna's divorce took place four months after the death of her two youngest children.

It was her faith and belief in God that has strengthened and encouraged her to share her story with others.

Towhanna has been reaching out to others in the Virginia, Maryland, and D.C. areas, empowering, encouraging, and inspiring people of all walks of life that **we indeed can do all things through Christ** who strengthens us!

For more information or book discussions, please email towhanna@gmail.com or go to www.towhannaboston.weebly.com.

About Kingdom Journey Press

Kingdom Journey Press, Inc. is a full-service publishing company specializing in providing customized services to support our clients from the conception of an idea to getting HIStory to the masses! Since the time of inception and in conjunction with our umbrella organization, Kingdom Journey Enterprises, we have become recognized globally for our ability to establish a unique presence, while building relationships with partners and clients consisting of current and aspiring writers, and ministry, business, and community organizations.

Our services include:

- Manuscript Evaluation
- Coaching for current and aspiring authors
- Editing
- Cover and Print Layout Design
- Print and E-Book Format
- Copyright and
- Worldwide Distribution
- Marketing and Sales Support

For more information, visit our website at www.kjpressinc.com.

www.ingramcontent.com/pod-product-compliance
Lightning Source LLC
LaVergne TN
LVHW041234080426
835508LV00011B/1197

* 9 7 8 0 9 8 9 0 8 7 8 3 4 *